Published by Flower Associates
Copyright (c) 2005 Lara M. Fares
Illustrator : Shireen Farah
Designer : Yasmeen Farah

All rights are reserved and no part of this publication may be reproduced, stored, transmitted in any form or by any means including electronic, mechanical photocopy without the prior written permisson of the copyright owner.

ISBN 0-9551768-0-8
ISBN 978-0-9551768-0-7
www.flowerassociates.co.uk

IT'S READY!

Edited by Lara M. Fares

These pictures are made by the children from **"The Speech, Language and Hearing Centre"**.

DEDICATION

This book is dedicated to my Father, who lost his speech during the last few years of his life. Over these painful years, I had time to think and realise how important it is to be able to communicate with fluency.

ACKNOWLEDGMENTS & THANKS

Last year I have come to a stage where I wanted to start working with Charities especially the ones involved with children. Fortunately Mr Dirk Flower (Child Psychologist) introduced me to a magical initiative.

This magical place is the "child" of Mrs Angela Harding and the only centre of it's kind in the UK who helps babies and children under 5 with hearing impairment or delay in speech, language and communication. This place works to integrate these children in normal schools and to help them live their lives with confidence and self esteem.

The centre is called : **"The Speech, Language and Hearing Centre"**, also known as **"Christopher Place"** and it has been registered as a charity in 1991.

Also, what makes this school very special is the way the staff and the environment in it support the whole family. Children as well as parents.

As I became more involved with the children in **"Christopher Place"**, the magic started to work on me, and I felt the need to support the school, and contribute to help the persons involved in

order to continue their amazing work.

As with all charities, they need regular donations and top ups of money. So I have decided to bring together this book of recipes, all sent to me by friends and relatives, and hopefully sell lots and lots of it.

I would like to thank deeply my friends and family for contributing in sending me recipes of their children's favourite meals and puddings, I thank my cousins Yasmeen and Shireen for the beautiful work they did. Their editing and artistic skills helped the making of the book.

And of course my husband Michael for his continuing support of my endeavours.

A special Thanks to another Magician, Daniel Radcliffe (the "Harry Potter" actor) for sending me his favourite desert. My children and I can't wait to try his recipe, I am sure you will too.

Finally I would like to thank all of you who choose to help **"Christopher Place"** by buying this book and I hope you enjoy trying all these Yummy recipes.

Lara M. FARES

Harry Potter star Daniel Radcliffe's raspberry and amaretti crunch cake

INGREDIENTS

Ready in 1 hr 20 mins. – 1 hr 30 mins.

Serves 6 people.

- 175g soft butter
- 175g golden caster sugar
- 3 eggs
- 140g self-raising flour
- 85g amaretti biscuits, roughly broken
- 250g punnet raspberries

To serve
- Icing sugar, to dust
- 142ml carton single cream

PROCEDURE

Preheat the oven to fan 140°C/conventional 160°C. Butter and base line a loose-bottomed 20cm round cake tin. Put the butter, caster sugar, eggs, flour and ground almonds into a large bowl. Beat using an electric hand whisk until all the ingredients are well blended.

Spread half the cake mixture in the lined tin. Scatter over half of the amaretti biscuits then a third of the raspberries. Very lightly press into the cake mixture.

Dollop dessertspoonfuls of the remaining cake mixture over the amaretti and raspberries and spread evenly. Scatter the remaining amaretti and half the remaining raspberries over the top. Bake for 55 - 60 mins., until a skewer inserted in the centre comes out clean.

Cool for 15 mins. in the tin. Run a knife round the edge and turn out. It will keep in a covered container in the fridge for up to 2 days.

To serve :

Remove from the fridge an hour before serving and lightly dust with icing sugar before bringing to the table. Serve with the remaining raspberries and a little single cream.

SAVOURY

SALADS
Aline's rice salad..................11
Nora's loubieh bil zeit............13
Julietta's lentil salad............15

VEGETARIAN
Carla's potatoes croquettes.......17
Jijo's mjadra......................19
Ghazwa's egg fried rice............21

PASTA
Noora's pasta......................23
Ismat's pasta pesto alla monica....25
Lara A's "orange pasta"
or pasta sauce napolitano..........27

HAM & SAUSAGE
Emma's ham endives.................29
Emma's tartiflette.................31
Jahnene's toad in the hole.........33

BEEF AND VEAL
Lynna's minced meat with rice......35
Anne marie's bolognese meat sauce..37
Shireen's spinach stew.............39
Mona's veal with lemon sauce.......41

CHICKEN
Youmna's ketchup chicken...........43
Hoda's chicken burger..............45
Elodie's chicken nuggets...........47
Oumayma's chicken
with mange-tout....................49
Raya's chicken stew................51
Mona's upside down chicken curry...53

SEAFOOD
Elodie's favourite salmon..........55
Carla's salmon
with spinach creamy sauce..........57
Rania's rice with prawns...........59

TABLE OF CONTENTS

Hoda's chocolate chip cookies..........63
Fifi's peanut butter cookies...............65
Hoda's chocolate cake.......................67
Mimi K's orange cake........................69
Lara A's yummy vanilla cake..............71
Tania's hummingbird cake.................73
Aline's marquise au chocolat.............75
Lara F's tiramisu................................77
Joannie's mousse au chocolat...........79
Emma's "pain perdu".........................81
Rima J's banana bread......................83
Mireille's banofie pie.........................85
Juliana's coconut biscuit balls...........87
Tania's cornflake crunch...................89
Tania's marshmallow crispies.............91
Joannie's pecan pie...........................93
Sirrine's almond cake........................95
Mimi's sticky toffee...........................97
Elena's poppy seed cake...................99
Yasmeen's crêpes sucrées................101
Leila's cake......................................103
Anne Marie's sponge cake...............105
Karen's cooked fruit salad...............107
Carla's tartare
of strawberries with basil................109
Zina's peach and raspberry
"clafoutis".......................................111

SWEET

SAVOURY

Aline's rice salad

INGREDIENTS

- 1kg small cooked shrimps
- 1 tea cup of boiled rice with 1 tsp of curry powder and
- 1 cube Knorr
- 1 tea cup of small pickles very thinly cut
- 1 cup of peeled, seeded and squeezed tomatoes, cut in cubes
- 1 cup of cucumbers cut in cubes

Sauce :
- 3 tbsps of lemon juice
- 1 small cup (coffee)
- olive oil
- 1 small cup of white vinegar
- Salt and white pepper to taste.

PROCEDURE

Mix all ingredients in a large bowl.

Refrigerate for one hour.

Serve.

Nora's loubie bil zeit

INGREDIENTS

- 1kg green beans
- 1 big onion (or 3 normal sized ones)
- 1 1/2 cup virgin olive oil
- 4 fresh peeled tomatoes
- 1 garlic (the entire thinghead)
- A pinch of salt

PROCEDURE

Wash the onion and chop it into squares.

Peel the garlic cloves.

Place them into a large casserole and cook them until they become golden.

Add the beans and mix carefully so as not to break the beans (toss them).

Add the salt and leave to cook for a few minutes.

Crush the tomatoes and add them to the beans. Proceed cooking until the beans become supple.

This should take roughly an hour. Add the rest of the oil and leave on the stove for a further 10 mins.

Julietta's lentils salad

INGREDIENTS

- 2 cups small onion
- 2 tbsps olive oil
- 1 pack of lentils, cleaned & rinsed
- 2 cans each : 1.2kg tinned plum tomatoes (peeled) pieces
- 1 cup of each : olive oil & boiling water
- 2 tbsps minced garlic
- 1 tsp of each : oregano, bay leaf, basil & thyme

PROCEDURE

Sauté the onions until soft and clear in 2 tablespoons olive oil.

Add all other ingredients and bring to boiling point. Simmer on low heat for 1 hour stirring occasionally.

Keep covered. Cook until liquid has evaporated and lentils are tender.

Transfer to glass bowl. Stir in : 3 tablespoons lemon juice, 2 teaspoons minced garlic & and salt and pepper to taste.

Remove bay leaf. Keep refrigerated and serve chilled. Add more lemon and garlic if desired.

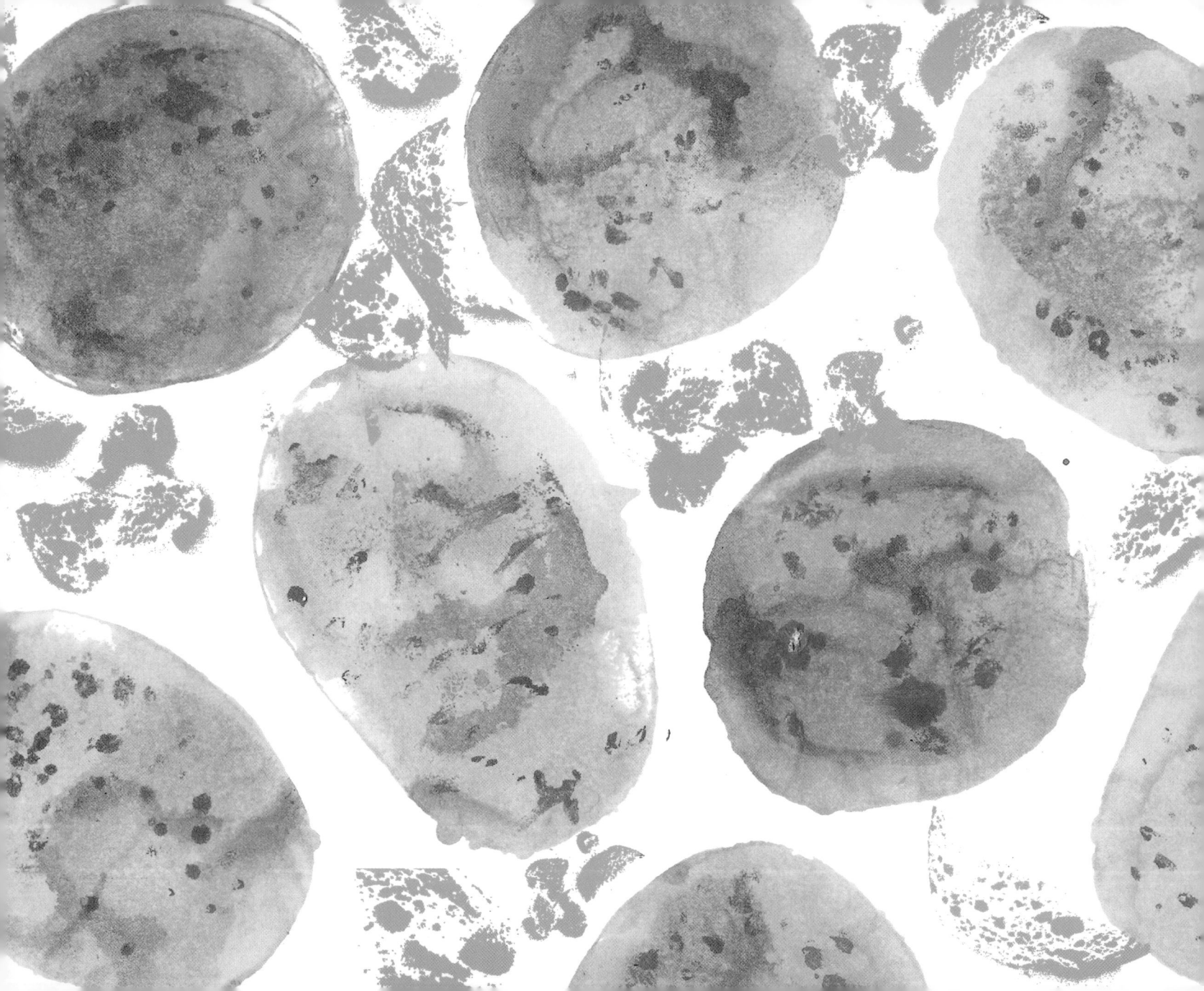

Carla's potatoes croquettes

INGREDIENTS

- 1kg potatoes
- 2 eggs yolks
- 20g butter
- 75g flour
- 60g grated cheddar cheese
- 2 eggs
- 2 tbsps milk
- 100g breadcrumbs
- Corn oil for frying
- Mozzarella cheese cut into cubes

PROCEDURE

Peel and boil the potatoes. Drain and mash with a fork, then add the egg yolks, the butter and the grated cheddar cheese. Mix well and refrigerate for 30 mins.

Flour your hands and take one tbsp of potatoes and shape it into a cylinder, roll it in flour, then make a hole in the centre and put a cube of mozzarella cheese in it. Reshape to cover the hole.

Mix the eggs with the milk, dip the potato croquettes into the mixture, and roll them in the breadcrumbs.

Put the croquettes on a tray and refrigerate for about 30 mins.

Heat up the oil in a frying pan, and fry the croquettes until golden brown.

Jijo's mjadra

INGREDIENTS

Serves 4 people.

- 2 cups rice
- 1 cup green lentils
- 4 onions (peeled and fried)
- 1/4 cup of vegetable oil
- 4 cups water
- 1 tsp salt
- 1 tsp pepper

PROCEDURE

Wash lentils.

Put water in a pot, add the lentils. Let them boil over medium heat, then reduce heat and cook for 30 mins.

Add the rice, salt and pepper to taste.

Cover and boil over low heat for 20 mins.

Ghazwa's egg fried rice

INGREDIENTS

- 3 eggs
- 3 tbsps vegetable oil
- 450g cooked rice*
- 2 spring onions (finely chopped)
- 115g frozen peas

PROCEDURE

* Soak raw rice in water for a short time before cooking.

Lightly beat the eggs with a pinch of salt and a few pieces of spring onions.

Heat the oil in a frying pan and lightly scramble the eggs.

Add the cooked rice and stir to make sure that each grain of rice is separated. Add salt, spring onions and the peas.

Noora's pasta

INGREDIENTS

- 1/2 packet of spaghetti
- 3 tbsps olive oil
- 1 large onion (chopped)
- 3 garlic cloves (crushed)
- 1/2 cup pitted olives
- 1 can chopped tomatoes
- Fresh basil

PROCEDURE

Bring pasta to boil (read instructions on packet), drain and set aside.

Meanwhile, heat olive oil in separate pan; add onions, garlic, tomatoes and olives. Stir on a medium heat until onions are tender.

Add to pasta, sprinkle with fresh basil, and serve.

Ismat's pasta pesto alla monica

INGREDIENTS

(A)
- 2 big bunches of fresh basil
- 1 big bunch of fresh parsley
- 4 tbsps of pine kernels (pinenuts)
- 2 glasses of olive oil
- 100g grated parmesan
- 1 garlic clove
- Salt

(B)
- 1 big large spoon of mascarpone or cottage cheese
- Tagliatelli or linguini pasta
- 50g of green beans, boiled al dente
- 6 baby potatoes, boiled al dente

PROCEDURE

Place all the (A) ingredients in the mixer, mix and pour into serving plate.
Never heat pesto sauce.

Add the mascarpone or cottage cheese to the pesto sauce with a little drop of boiling water. "You will get a beautiful green colour."

Cook the pasta, preferably Linguini or Tagliatelli.

Sieve the pasta and add it over the light green sauce.

Decorate with the beans and potatoes.

I suggest you double or triple the quantity in (A) and place the mixture in little jars and freeze. "Always come in handy."

Lara A's "orange pasta" or pasta sauce napolitano

INGREDIENTS

- 1 tomato can (chopped tomatoes in sauce)
- 1 medium onion (finely chopped)
- 1 celery stalk (finely chopped)
- 1 big carrot (finely chopped)
- 3 tbsps olive oil
- 1 cube organic chicken stock (or fresh stock)
- 3 tbsps of single cream
- Salt and pepper to taste

PROCEDURE

Fry onion, carrot and celery with the olive oil until softened.

Add chicken stock, chopped tomatoes in sauce, some water and seasoning.

Cover and simmer for about 20 mins. or until cooked.

Turn off the heat and put the sauce in a mixer.

Finally add the cream and taste...

Emma's ham endives

INGREDIENTS

- 4 white endives (chicory)

Béchamel Sauce:
- 75 g of butter
- 4 tbsps of flour
- 2 cups of milk
- 4 slices of ham
- Parmesan cheese,
- Salt and pepper.

PROCEDURE

Melt the butter in a pan.
Add the flour stirring it all the time.
Add the milk little by little to do the béchamel sauce.
Add the seasoning.

Roll each endive in a slice of ham.
Put the rolls in a Pyrex.

Pour the béchamel on top.
Then the parmesan cheese.
Put in oven for 40 mins. at 180°C.

Emma's tartiflette

INGREDIENTS

- 4 potatoes
- 1 pack of raclette cheese
- Salt, pepper
- Ham or bacon.

PROCEDURE

Cut the potatoes, the cheese and the bacon in small pieces.

Mix everything in a Pyrex.

Put in the oven, at 180°C with 2 tablespoons of water for 20 - 30 mins.

Serve with crudités (raw vegetables) for a healthy dish!

Jahnene's toad in the hole

INGREDIENTS

- 8 - 10 nice sausages grilled
- 2 x 40 ml water or milk
- 100g flour
- 2 eggs
- Salt and pepper

PROCEDURE

Mix all the above Ingredients and let it rest (the longer the better) Place vegetable oil or dripping in a roasting tray.

Heat the oil or dripping so that it is so hot it begins to smoke in the oven or over the gas hob.

Pour in the mix and the grilled sausages.

Place inside the oven at 205°C.

Bake until cooked.

Serve with gravy and vegetables.

Lynna's minced meat with rice soup

INGREDIENTS

- 1 Medium Onion (Chopped)
- 1 large potato (Chopped)
- 2 large carrots scraped and chopped
- 2 Medium fresh tomatoes cut into small pieces
- 1/2 cup pudding rice
- Mince meat as desired
- Salt & pepper

PROCEDURE

Fry the chopped onion until tender. Add the minced meat and bring to boil.

Reduce the heat and simmer until meat is cooked and tender.

Add the carrots, rice, tomatoes and all of the ingredients.

Mix thoroughly and simmer partially covered, for about 20 mins. or until all vegetables are cooked and tender.

Serve hot.

Anne-Marie's bolognese meat sauce

INGREDIENTS

- 25g butter
- 50ml olive oil
- 1 onion (finely chopped)
- 1 carrot (finely chopped)
- 1 celery stick (finely chopped)
- 500g lean, minced beef
- 1 clove of garlic (finely chopped)
- 150ml red wine
- 400g chopped plum tomatoes with their juice (from can)
- 1 bay leaf
- 1/4 tsp fresh thyme leaves

PROCEDURE

Heat the butter and oil in a heavy saucepan. Add the onion, and cook over moderate heat for 3 – 4 mins. Stir in the carrot, celery and garlic. Cook for 3 – 4 mins. more.

Add the beef, and crumble it into the vegetables with a fork. Stir until the meat loses its red colour. Season to taste with salt and pepper.

Pour in the wine, raise heat slightly, and cook until the liquid evaporates : 3 – 4 mins.

Stir in the tomatoes with their juice and the herbs. Bring the sauce to boiling point. Lower the heat and simmer uncovered for 1 – 11/2, stirring occasionally.

Taste the seasoning before serving.

Shireen's spinach stew

INGREDIENTS

Serves 4 people.

- 1kg spinach (washed and chopped)
- 1/4kg minced beef
- 1 onion (chopped)
- 4 garlic cloves (crushed)
- 1/2 bunch fresh coriander (chopped)
- 1 tsp salt
- Allspice and black pepper
- 1/4 cup pine nuts (fried)
- Bicarbonate of soda

PROCEDURE

Boil water ; add bicarbonate of soda and spinach. Allow to boil over for 3 mins.

Remove, and wash well. Put aside.

Fry onions, add meat, and salt and pepper to taste.

Stir in coriander, garlic and spinach.

Mix well, add 1 cup of water.

Leave them to boil on medium heat for 20 mins.

Add pine nuts and accompany with cooked basmati rice.

Mona's veal with lemon sauce

INGREDIENTS

- 4 thinly sliced medium sized veal escallops (unbraided)
- 1 tbsp flour
- 1/2 cup olive oil
- 100g butter
- 1/2 cup sliced shallots
- 1 bunch fresh thyme
- 1/2 cup lemon juice

PROCEDURE

Toss veal with flour and put on the side.

Heat 1/2 of the butter and olive oil in a pan, add veal slices, and stir on a medium heat until golden brown, and put on the side.

Heat remaining butter and shallots until tender. Add thyme and lemon juice, and stir for 2 mins. on a medium heat, and serve over the veal.

Serving suggestion :
Accompany with basmati rice cooked with peas and pine nuts.

Youmna's ketchup chicken

INGREDIENTS

Dead easy to do and always a favourite…

Take random pieces of chicken, put them in an ovenproof dish and marinate them with the following sauce:
Worcestershire Sauce (a good dash)
Mild mustard (to taste)
Salt and pepper
And a generous amount of….KETCHUP!

PROCEDURE

Place the dish in a medium hot oven and bake, turning regularly until the chicken is cooked.

This is an ideal dish for picnics, if done ahead to allow the chicken to cool ; or can also be eaten hot at home with a nice potato salad or baked potatoes.

The longer you allow for the chicken to be marinated, the better it will be.

Note that no quantities are given…because the marinade was always done on "inspiration"….Believe me, it works…

Hoda's chicken hamburger

INGREDIENTS

- 1 whole chicken
- 1 medium onion
- 1 1/2 tsps salt
- 1/2 tsp black pepper
- 4 big hamburger breads

PROCEDURE

Clean the chicken very well. Extract the bones and mince the chicken.

Chop the onion finely ; add it to the chicken, plus the salt and pepper.

Make big round balls. Flatten each ball into a paddy, grill it and put it in the burger bread.
You can also add, lettuce, tomatoes, pickles, tomato ketchup, mustard or mayonnaise.

Serve hot with French fries.

Elodie's chicken nuggets

INGREDIENTS

- 3 chicken breasts (skinless)
- 2 eggs (beaten lightly)
- Homemade breadcrumbs (Swedish Krisprolls blended in a food processor)
- Flour (mixed with salt and pepper)
- Vegetable oil for frying

PROCEDURE

Cut chicken into small pieces, and flatten by beating with a meat tenderiser.

Coat each piece in flour, and then dip into egg, followed by breadcrumbs.

Preheat oil in deep saucepan and fry nuggets until golden brown.

Oumayma's chicken with mange-tout

INGREDIENTS

- 6 packs chicken breast (cut in cubes)
- 1 pack mange-tout [French beans] (cut in 3 thin strips)
- Ginger (finely grated)
- Soya sauce
- Sesame oil
- Garlic (finely grated)
- Onion (in rings)
- 1/2 bottle oyster sauce

PROCEDURE

Marinate the chicken with ginger, Soya sauce, sesame oil, garlic and allow marinating for 2 – 3 hours.

Fry the onion (half done). Remove, and fry the mange-tout (half done).

Fry the chicken with the sauce for approx. 10 mins., using the same oil.

Add the oyster sauce at the end. Boil for about 2 mins. and serve.

Serve with plain basmati or pudding rice.

Basmati rice :
Soak with boiling water for 10 min (1 cup rice = 1 1/2 cup boiling water).

Raya's chicken stew

INGREDIENTS

- 1 whole chicken
- 3 medium potatoes
- 4 carrots
- 12 small onions or shallots
- 2 heaped tbsps flour,
- salt and pepper
- 1/2 cup cooking oil

PROCEDURE

Clean the chicken well, paste the inside with lemon, and boil until well cooked.

Leave to cool and take off the bones.

Reserve the bouillon.

Peel the potatoes and cut them up in chunks, peel and dice the carrots and dice, peel the onions and keep them whole.

Heat the oil in a pot ; add the vegetables which you will sprinkle with the flour, salt and pepper and keep stirring until vegetables are brown.

Add the bouillon little by little while stirring, add the chicken, cover and simmer for 30 mins., or until vegetables are tender.

Serve with rice.

Mona's upside down chicken curry

INGREDIENTS

- 3 – 4 spoons cooking oil
- 1kg chicken (boneless, skinless and cubed)
- 2 large onions (finely chopped)
- 6 garlic cloves (crushed)
- Fresh ginger (grated)
- 3 spoons curry powder
- 1 1/2 cups basmati rice (washed and soaked in water)
- 1 can corn
- 4 – 5 spoons raisins

PROCEDURE

Heat oil, and fry onions and chicken.

Add salt (to taste), curry powder, garlic and ginger, until chicken is cooked, and onions are golden brown.

Add rice and corn, stir over, and add 3 cups of water.

Bring to a boil, and then reduce heat until rice is cooked.

Turn over upside down pan onto a plate, sprinkle with butter fried raisins.

Elodie's favourite salmon

INGREDIENTS

- Salmon fillet
- Pesto sauce
- Lemon juice
- Breadcrumbs

PROCEDURE

Place salmon fillet on baking tray, and sprinkle with lemon juice.

Coat the top with pesto. Cover the top with breadcrumbs, and bake until breadcrumbs are golden brown.

Serving suggestion :
Serve with (or on top of) a carrot and potato mash.

Carla's salmon with spinach creamy sauce

INGREDIENTS

- 4 salmon steaks / fillets
- 200g spinach
- 1 bunch watercress
- 2 carrots (chopped in cubes)
- 1 small onion (finely chopped)
- 50g cream cheese
- 1/2 a lemon

PROCEDURE

Coat salmon steaks with olive oil, add salt and pepper.

Place salmon steaks under grill (or in foil in preheated oven for approx. 20 mins.).

Sauce:

Fry onion and carrots in olive oil, until lightly brown.

Add spinach and watercress and cook for approx. 15 mins.

Blend with a hand blender and add cream cheese.

Add lemon juice, salt, pepper and nutmeg to taste.

Place salmon on a bed of cooked basmati rice and pour sauce over it. Garnish with a sprig of watercress.

Rania's rice with prawns

INGREDIENTS

- 1kg prawns
- 2 cloves of garlic smashed
- 4 diced chives
- 1 onion chopped
- 3 large fresh tomatoes peeled and chopped
- 2 cups of tomato sauce
- 1 green pepper chopped
- 1 red pepper chopped
- 2 tsps of salt
- 1 tsp of pepper
- 1 tsp of curry
- Parsley for decoration

PROCEDURE

Stir fry onion in Vegetable oil.

Add curry, then chives followed by peppers and garlic.

Add the prawns when all above ingredients are soft.

Add tomatoes and tomato sauce at the end.

Then add salt and pepper to taste. Stir well.

Garnish with parsley and serve with basmati rice.

SWEET

Hoda's chocolate chip cookies

INGREDIENTS

- 1 cup margarine or butter
- 1 large egg
- 3/4 cup packed brown sugar
- 3/4 cup granulated sugar
- 2 1/4 cups all purpose flour (if you use self raising omit baking soda and salt)
- 1 tsp baking soda
- 1/2 tsp salt
- 1 cup coarsely chopped nuts
- 2 cups chocolate chips

PROCEDURE

Heat oven to 190°C.

Mix sugar, butter and eggs in large bowl.

Stir in flour, baking soda and salt (dough will be tough).

Stir in nuts and chocolate chips.

Using a rounded tablespoon, place the dough onto a non-greased cookie sheet. Make sure to keep the servings 2" apart.

Bake 8 - 10 mins. or until light brown (centres will be soft).

Allow to cool slightly then remove from cookie sheet. Cool on wire rack.

Fifi's peanut butter cookies

INGREDIENTS

- 1/2 cup granulated white sugar
- 1/2 cup brown sugar
- 1/2 cup butter
- 1/2 cup peanut butter
- 1 egg
- 1 1/4 cups all purpose flour
- 3/4 tsp baking soda
- 1/2 tsp baking powder
- 1/4 tsp salt

PROCEDURE

Mix together both brown and white sugars, then add the butter, peanut butter and egg and mix in.

Add flour, baking soda, baking powder and salt and mix in. Cover mixture and refrigerate for 3 hours.

Preheat oven to 375°C.

Prepare a baking tray and line with a baking sheet.

Shape the dough into tablespoon sized balls and place them on the tray spaced out.

Bake for 10 mins.

Leave to cool on a cooling rack.

Hoda's chocolate cake

INGREDIENTS

- 2 cups floor
- 2 cups sugar
- 2 eggs
- 2/3 cup yoghurt
- 1 tsp vanilla
- 1 tsp baking powder
- 1 tsp baking soda
- 1/2 cup butter
- 3 tbsps cooking cocoa

PROCEDURE

Heat oven to 175°C.

Grease 9" round cake tin.

Melt the butter with cocoa.

Mix sugar, vanilla & yoghurt until fluffy, blend in eggs, combine cocoa mix, flour, baking powder and baking soda, blend thoroughly.

Pour into bowl.

Bake for 30 - 35 mins. Allow to cool it for 10 mins.

Remove from tin and cool on a wire tray.

Mimi K's orange cake

INGREDIENTS

- 4 eggs
- 1 cup of Mazola oil
- 1 1/2 cups of orange juice
- A pinch of salt
- A pinch of Vanilla
- 3 cups of flour
- 3 tsps of baking powder
- 1 tbsp Cointreau
- 2 tbsps of hot water

PROCEDURE

Mix all ingredients together ; bake in the oven for approximately one hour at 175°C.

Once out of the oven, while still hot pour over the cake 5 teaspoons of honey.

Lara A's yummy vanilla cake

INGREDIENTS

- 125g butter
- 3/4 cup of milk
- 3 eggs
- 1 tbsp of vanilla essence
- 1 cup of castor sugar
- 1 1/2 cups of self raising flour

PROCEDURE

Grease a deep 19cm square cake pan.

Combine butter and milk in saucepan, stir constantly over heat until butter is melted. Remove from heat and cool to room temperature.

Beat eggs and essence in small bowl with electric mixer until thick and creamy : add sugar gradually, beat until dissolved.

Transfer into a large bowl.

Stir in half the sifted flour and half the butter mixture, then the remaining flour and butter mixture.

Pour in pan and bake in moderate oven for about 45 mins.
When cold, sift icing sugar over the cake.

Tania's hummingbird cake

INGREDIENTS

- 450g crushed pineapple in syrup (from can)
- 1 cup plain flour
- 1/2 cup self raising flour
- 1/2 tsp bicarbonate of soda
- 1/2 tsp ground cinnamon
- 1/2 tsp ground ginger
- 1 cup firmly packed brown sugar
- 1/2 cup dissipated coconut
- 1 cup mashed banana
- 2 lightly beaten eggs
- 3/4 cup vegetable oil

- 100g melted butter
- 200g Philadelphia cream cheese
- 1 tsp vanilla essence
- 1/2 cup icing sugar

PROCEDURE

Preheat oven to moderate temperature.

Drain pineapple over medium bowl, pressing with spoon to extract as much syrup as possible.

Reserve 1/4 cup syrup.

Sift flour, soda, spices and sugar into a large bowl using wooden spoon. Stir in drained pineapple, reserved syrup, coconut, banana, eggs and oil. Pour into prepared pan.

Bake in moderate oven for about 40 mins. Let cake stand for 5 mins. Turn cake top side to cool.

Spread cold cake with cream cheese frosting.

Beat butter, cream cheese and vanilla in a small bowl with electric mixer until light and fluffy, gradually beating in icing sugar.

Cream cheese frosting

Spread the mixture over the cake.

Aline's marquise au chocolat

INGREDIENTS

Ready in 30 mins. + 15 mins. for the cream
Do it a day in advance.

Serves 8 to 10 people.

Marquise:
- 250g chocolate
- 125g butter
- 3 eggs
- 100g glazed sugar
- Vanilla or coffee (pinch)

Crème anglaise:
- 250ml of milk
- 2 eggs (yellow yolks)
- 50g sugar
- Vanilla or coffee

PROCEDURE

Melt the chocolate at low heat in 3 tablespoons of water. When melted, remove from heat.

Work the butter with a spatula to soften. Do not heat it in order to keep its aroma.

Separate yolks from whites. Add yolks one by one in the cream butter, then add the glazed sugar, and work the dough fully.

Mix the melted chocolate, perfumed with the vanilla or the coffee. Mix it very well. Let it cool down completely before adding the mix, whisk the egg whites until stiff but not dry.

Pour it in a Pyrex, buttered. Put it in the fridge for 10 hours approximately.

Prepare a vanilla or coffee crème anglaise : pour the boiling milk on the yellows of the eggs and the sugar. Thicken at low fire by stirring non stop. Remove from heat just before boiling point.

Let it cool.

To remould, soak the mould few seconds in hot water. Turn upside down in a plate. Embrace it with the crème anglaise.

Lara F's tiramisu

INGREDIENTS

Serves 6 to 8 people.

- 3 eggs, separated
- 450g, or 2 cups Mascarpone cheese, at room temperature
- 1 sachet of vanilla sugar
- 175ml strong black coffee (cold)
- 120ml Kahlua or other coffee-flavoured liqueur
- 18 savoiardi (Italian sponge fingers) sifted cocoa powder and grated bittersweet chocolate, to finish.

PROCEDURE

The name of this popular dessert translates as "pick me up", which is said to derive from the fact that it is so good that it literally makes you swoon when you eat it. There are many, many versions, and the recipe can be adapted to suit your own taste - you can vary the amount of mascarpone, eggs, sponge fingers, coffee and liqueur.

Put the egg whites in a grease-free bowl and whisk with an electric mixer until stiff and in peaks.

Mix the mascarpone, vanilla sugar and egg yolks in a separate large bowl and whisk with the electric mixer until evenly combined. Fold in the egg whites, then put a few spoonfuls of the mixture in the bottom of a large serving bowl and spread it out evenly.

Mix the coffee and liqueur together in a shallow dish. Dip a sponge finger in the mixture, turn it quickly so that it becomes saturated but does not disintegrate, and place it on top of the mascarpone in the bowl. Add five more dipped sponge fingers, placing them side by side.

Spoon in about one-third of the remaining mixture and spread it out. Make more layers in the same way, ending with mascarpone. Level the surface, and then sift cocoa powder all over. Cover and chill overnight. Before serving, sprinkle with cocoa and grated chocolate.

Joannie's mousse au chocolat

INGREDIENTS

- 7 eggs
- 400g bitter chocolate (60 or 70% cacao)
- 1/2 cup of strong coffee
- Pinch of salt

PROCEDURE

Melt the chocolate with the coffee in a bain-marie and set aside. Separate the yellow and white of eggs.

Beat the whites into stiff peaks and set aside. Mix the lightly beaten egg yolks into the melted chocolate.

Mix one third of the stiff egg whites into the chocolate and egg yolk mixture.

Mix well. Then delicately fold this chocolate mixture into the rest of the egg whites, folding the whites from underneath into the mixture.

Do not beat or stir vigorously. When the mousse is homogenous put it into a pretty bowl and set in fridge.

After 3 hours it will be ready to serve.

Emma's "pain perdu"

INGREDIENTS

- 4 slices of bread
- 2 eggs
- 1 cup of milk
- 2 tbsps of brown sugar
- 2 tsps of vanilla
- Butter for cooking
- Brown sugar to sprinkle

PROCEDURE

Beat the eggs with the milk, the sugar and the vanilla in a soup dish. Put the bread to soak in that mixture, when the bread is well drenched fry in a pan with a little butter.

Sprinkle sugar on the baked "pain perdu" and serve warm. Accompany with a banana (squashed on top) it's an easy and balanced breakfast.

Rima J's banana bread

INGREDIENTS

- 125g of butter
- 1 tsp of vanilla
- 3/4 cup of caster sugar
- 2 eggs
- 1 cup of 3 mashed bananas
- 3/4 cup (self raising) flour.
- 3/4 cup plain flour.
- 1/2 tsp bicarbonate of soda.
- 1/2 cup chopped walnuts

PROCEDURE

Preheat fan oven to 250°C.

Cream the butter, vanilla and sugar until fluffy.

Add the eggs one at a time and beat until well mixed.

Mix the self raising flour, plain flour, bicarbonate of soda together. Then sift them.

Stir in half the bananas and walnuts to half the dry ingredients mixture and stir.

Then stir in the other half.

Place in a long cake pan and cook between 45 mins. to 1 hour.

Mireille's banofie pie

INGREDIENTS

- 2 cans sweetened condensed milk
- 450g digestive biscuits
- 4 bananas
- Whipped cream
- Chocolate flakes or chocolate shavings
- Sprinkle of cinnamon
- Spring form dish or pie dish

PROCEDURE

Place the sweetened condensed milk in a pan letting the water reach it half way up the can.

Bring the water to a boil and let it simmer for 3 hours.

Turn the cans upside down after an hour and a half. This allows the milk to caramelize and become very thick... if it doesn't and is still runny when served, add to the cooking time.

Alternatively, you can place the tins in a pressure cooker filled half way up and let it cook for 40 mins. Don't worry ; the tins won't burst in either method of cooking.

Place the digestive biscuits in a food processor and mix until you have a fine powdery substance.

Place them in a cheesecake tin and mix them with melted butter with a sprinkle of cinnamon until they form a nice solid base for the pie.

Juliana's coconut biscuit balls

INGREDIENTS

- 1 packet of tea-rich biscuits
- 1 box of condensed milk nestle
- 2 tbsps of cacao
- 1 bag of coconut powder

PROCEDURE

Grind biscuits in food processor.

Mix milk and cacao in a bowl.

Add biscuits to milk mixture.

Make dough.

Work the balls into the size you desire, then roll them in the coconut powder.

Tania's cornflake crunch

INGREDIENTS

- 225g plain chocolate
- 3 tbsps golden or maple syrup
- 50g margarine
- 100g corn flakes

PROCEDURE

Grease a 20cm square tin with a little butter or margarine on kitchen paper. Grease the inside well, but do not leave too much butter.

Break the chocolate into a large pan. Add the syrup and margarine. Heat the pan, gently stirring all the time.

When the chocolate has melted. Add the corn flakes, and stir them well. Make sure that they are coated all over with chocolate.

Spoon the mixture into the tin. Gently smooth the top with the back of the spoon. Try not to crush the corn flakes.

Put the tin in the fridge for the chocolate to set - it will take about 2 hours to set. Use a sharp knife to cut.

Tania's marshmallow crispies

INGREDIENTS

- 100g wrapped toffees or slab toffee
- 100g margarine
- 100g marshmallow
- 100g rice crispies

PROCEDURE

Grease the square tin (If you are using a slab of toffee, put it in a plastic bag and break it up with a rolling pin).

Put the toffee, margarine and marshmallow into a large pan. Melt them very gently over a low heat, stirring all the time.

When everything has melted and blended together, take the pan off the heat. Gently stir in the rice crispies.

Spoon the mixture into the tin and press it gently with the back of a metal spoon. Leave the mixture to set, and then cut it up.

Joannie's pecan pie

INGREDIENTS

- 9 inch pie tin with 1 inch ridge
- 4 tbsps flour
- 5 tbsps melted butter
- 1 cup corn syrup or golden cane syrup
- 1/2 cup black strap molasses (found in health food shops)
- 1/2 cup maple syrup
- 5 eggs
- Salt
- 1 generous tbsp whiskey
- 2 cups shelled pecans

For the Pâte Brisée:
- 200g flour
- 100g butter
- Pinch of salt
- 1/2 cup of cold water

PROCEDURE

First the pâte brisée :
Put the flour, butter salt and water in a Magimix.

Process until a ball is formed.

Flour the marble top and roll out the dough, large enough to cover your pie tin plus the vertical ridge.

Be careful when transferring to the pie tin not to rip the dough, as the batter is quite liquid.

For the batter :
In a mixing bowl put the sugar, flour, syrups and molasses and mix.

Then add five well beaten eggs and continue mixing.

Now add the salt, whiskey and melted butter.

Mix thoroughly.

Pour the filling into the pie tin that has been lined with the unbaked pastry (pâte brisée).

Now add the pecan halves, directly in the pie tin, placing them close together so they cover the filling.

Bake the pie in a moderate oven for 35 - 45 mins. until the filling is set, i.e. when pricked with a toothpick it is not runny.

Sirrine's almond cake

INGREDIENTS

- 100g soft tub margarine
- 50g soft brown sugar
- 2 eggs
- 175g self raising flour
- 1 tsp baking powder
- 4 tbsps milk
- 2 tbsps runny honey
- 50g flaked almonds

Syrup:
- 150g runny honey
- 2 tbsps lemon juice

PROCEDURE

Grease an 18cm round cake tin (or pan) and line with baking parchment.

Place the margarine, brown sugar, eggs, flour, baking powder, milk and honey in a large mixing bowl and beat well with a wooden spoon for about one minute until all the ingredients are thoroughly mixed together.

Spoon into the prepared tin, level the surface with the back of a spoon or a knife and sprinkle with the almonds.

Bake in a preheated oven 180°C for about 50 mins., or until the cake is well risen.

Meanwhile, make the syrup – combine the honey and lemon juice in a small saucepan and simmer until the syrup starts to coat the back of a spoon.

As soon as the cake comes out of the oven, pour the syrup, allowing it to seep into the middle of the cake.

Leave the cake to cool for at least 2 hours before slicing.

Mimi's sticky toffee

INGREDIENTS

- 60g softened butter
- 175g granulated sugar
- 250g flour
- 1 tsp baking powder
- 1 egg
- 170g stoned dates
- 280ml boiling water
- 1 tsp bicarbonate of soda
- 1 tsp vanilla essence

- 80g brown sugar
- 45g butter
- 2 tbsps double cream

PROCEDURE

Cream together the butter and sugar. Sift the flour and baking powder. Beat whisked egg into the creamed mixture with some flour. Continue beating for a minute before adding the rest of the flour.

Flour the dates lightly and chop finely. Pour the boiling water over them. Mix in the soda and vanilla essence. Add mixture to the batter and blend well. Turn into a buttered cake tin (30cm).

For the toffee coating, heat the sugar and butter cream. Simmer for 3 mins.

Pour over the hot cake allowing toffee to get into the cake with the aid of a spatula/fork. (Mimi's touch again!)

Place under grill just before serving.

Serve with vanilla ice cream.

Elena's poppy seed cake

INGREDIENTS

- 1 cup butter
- 1 cup sugar
- 6 egg yolks
- 6 egg whites
- 2 tsps almond or vanilla extracts
- 2 cups flour (self-raising)
- 1 tsp salt
- 1 tsp baking soda
- 1 tsp baking powder
- 1 cup soured cream
- 1 cup poppy seeds
- 1/2 cup honey for glazing

PROCEDURE

Cream the butter and sugar till fluffy.

Beat in egg yolks, 1 at a time.

Add the almond (or vanilla) extract.

Sift the flour, salt and baking soda together and fold them into the butter mixture in turns with the sour cream.

Beat the egg whites until stiff. Fold into the batter.

Fold in the poppy seeds.

Pour batter into a prepared pan. Bake in the centre of a preheated oven at 175°C for about 45 mins., until a toothpick comes out clean when poked into the centre.

Let cool about 10 mins. then glaze by pouring the melted honey on top.

Remove from pan only when completely cooled.

Yasmeen's crêpes sucrées

INGREDIENTS

- 2 cups flour
- 3 eggs + 2 yellow
- 3 1/2 cups hot milk
- 1 pinch of salt
- 2 tbsps of powder sugar

PROCEDURE

Mix the flour and the eggs, including the yolks.

Slowly mix the milk, stirring as you pour.

Finally add the salt and sugar and miss well.

Pass it through the strainer.

Leila's cake

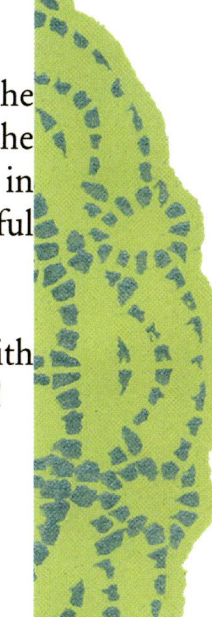

INGREDIENTS

- 5 eggs
- 2 cups of sugar
- 3 cups flour
- 1 cup melted butter (250g)
- 1 cup of milk
- Lime zest
- 1 tsp of Baking Powder
- 2 tsps of Cacao powder (optional to make a marble cake)

PROCEDURE

Beat the eggs with the sugar and the lemon zest.

Add the flour, the milk and the melted and continue to stir.

Pour the mixture in a buttered and floured tin.

Put in the oven for 45 mins. preheated at 200/220°C.

Option marble cake :
Same preparation.
Pour the 3/4 of the mixture in the tin and mix the 1/4 left with the cacao powder before pouring in the tin : You will have beautiful chocolate marbling.

Enjoy with your family or with friends, at breakfast, or for tea!

Anne-Marie's sponge cake

INGREDIENTS

Covered with chocolate and a strawberry filling

- 6 eggs
- 250g granulated sugar
- 1 tsp vanilla extract
- 1 tsp grated lemon zest
- 125g self raising flour, sifted
- 90g unsalted butter, melted
- 200g strawberry jam
- 300g milk chocolate

PROCEDURE

Preheat an oven to 180°C.

Butter a cake pan and line the bottom with baking parchment.

Place the eggs and sugar in the bowl, set the bowl over hot water, and whisk for a few minutes with an electric mixer until warm to the touch.

Remove the bowl from the hot water and beat on high spin for about 8 mins., until very thick and pale.

Stir in the vanilla and lemon zest with a spatula. Gently fold in half of the sifted flour, then the melted butter, and then the remaining flour.

Pour into the prepared pan, level the batter, and bake on the middle rack of the oven for about 30 mins., or until a toothpick inserted into the centre of the cake comes out clean.

Turn the cake out onto a rack to cool.

When cool, cut the sponge into 2 layers with a serrated knife.

Spoon the strawberry jam over the sponge layers, and assemble the cake.

Melt the chocolate in a bowl over hot water.

Cover the sponge with chocolate, then refrigerate until the chocolate settles.

Karen's cooked fruit salad

INGREDIENTS

- 2 cups strawberries
- 1 cup red currants
- 2 cups raspberries
- 1 cup blueberries
- 1 cup blackberries

PROCEDURE

To make in the berry season. A combination of the following fresh berries, not necessarily these exact fruits, but strawberries, raspberries and red currants are essential.

Cook half the strawberries, raspberries and red currants with 1/2 to 1 cup of sugar (to taste) and 1/2 cup of water until they give off their juice, usually for about 10 mins. Then add all the other fruits and cook only for 3 mins. Pour into a glass bowl and serve when cooled into individual bowls.

Carla's tartare of strawberries with basil

INGREDIENTS

- 500g strawberries
- 1/2 a sweet apple
- 1/2 a lemon
- 50g pine nuts
- 5ml olive oil
- 50g sugar
- 8 basil leaves

PROCEDURE

Grill the pine nuts in a teflon pan (no oil).

Mix the olive oil with the pine nuts, the sugar, and the basil leaves. Process in a food processor, until smooth and creamy in texture.

Peel and cut the apple into small cubes.

Delicately mix the apple, strawberries (cut into small pieces), and lemon, and add the pine nut mixture to it.

Refrigerate slightly, and serve in pretty couples.

Zina's peach and raspberry "clafoutis"

INGREDIENTS

Serves 6 people.

- 150g raspberry
- 2 ripe peaches
- 2 eggs
- 100g self-rising flour
- 60g caster sugar
- 2 tbsps honey
- 1 tsp baking powder
- 5 tbsps groundnut oil
- 2 tbsps rum or cognac
- Icing sugar to decorate

PROCEDURE

Preheat the oven to 220°C.

In a bowl, mix together the sugar with the eggs and the honey until you get a smooth mixture.

Add flour and baking powder and mix well.

Add oil and rum and mix all the ingredients together.

Peel and dice one peach. Add it to the mixture.

Peel and slice the other peach and keep it aside.

Grease a ceramic mould (22 cm diameter) with butter.

Pour the mixture over the mould and arrange peach slices and raspberry on top.

Bake for 20 - 25 mins., until golden on top.

Serve warm, with a light sprinkle of icing sugar.